MINING IN AMERICA

MINING AND THE ENVIRONMENT

BY EMMA KAISER

Core Library

An Imprint of Abdo Publishing

abdobooks.com

Cover image: The Morenci copper mine in Arizona is one of the largest copper mines in North America. But some activists are concerned with the impact copper mining has on the environment.

abdobooks.com

Published by Abdo Publishing, a division of ABDO, PO Box 398166, Minneapolis, Minnesota 55439.

Printed in the United States of America, North Mankato, Minnesota.
052023
092023

THIS BOOK CONTAINS RECYCLED MATERIALS

Cover Photo: Hanna Steadman/Shutterstock Images
Interior Photos: The Washington Post/Getty Images, 4–5; Cable Hoover/Gallup Independent/AP Images, 7; Jon G. Fuller/VWPics/AP Images, 9; Theo Stroomer/Stringer/Getty Images News/Getty Images, 12–13, 45; George Rose/Getty Images News/Getty Images, 15; Eric Vance/EPA/Flickr, 18, 40; Malachi Jacobs/Shutterstock Images, 20–21; Thom Bridge/Independent Record/AP Images, 23; Red Line Editorial, 26, 37; Shutterstock Images, 28–29, 43; M L Pearson/Alamy, 31; Geoff Liesik/The Deseret News/AP Images, 33; Jim West/Alamy, 34–35

Editor: Angela Lim
Series Designer: Ryan Gale

Library of Congress Control Number: 2022949080

Publisher's Cataloging-in-Publication Data
Names: Kaiser, Emma, author.
Title: Mining and the Environment / by Emma Kaiser
Description: Minneapolis, Minnesota: Abdo Publishing Company, 2024 | Series: Mining in America | Includes online resources and index.
Identifiers: ISBN 9781098290962 (lib. bdg.) | ISBN 9781098277147 (ebook)
Subjects: LCSH: Mines and mining--Juvenile literature. | Mines and mineral resources--Juvenile literature. | American history--Juvenile literature. | Mining engineering--Juvenile literature. | United States--Juvenile literature.
Classification: DDC 622.0973--dc23

CONTENTS

DANGER
ABANDONED
URANIUM MINE
KEEP OUT
Ba'ha'dzid - Doo Ko'ne'na'adaa'da
NO
Building
Gathering
Playing
Corrals
Digging
AT MINES
Contact Navajo Superfund Program
for Information at 1-800-314-1846
or USEPA at 1-800-231-3075

CHAPTER ONE

MINING'S ENVIRONMENTAL AFTERMATH

The Northeast Church Rock Mine opened in New Mexico in 1967. It quickly became one of the highest-producing uranium mines in the state. Uranium is a metal used to make nuclear weapons. It also fuels nuclear power plants. Uranium is radioactive and can be difficult to contain. Exposure to uranium can lead to cancer and other harmful health effects.

On the morning of July 16, 1979, the dam at the mine failed. The dam held water that

Signs posted outside an abandoned uranium mine in the Navajo Nation warn people of radioactive contamination.

was used in the mining process. Because of its contact with uranium, the water had become radioactive. When the dam broke, 94 million gallons (355 million L) of uranium wastewater washed into the nearby Puerco River. Employees noticed the leak in the dam at 6:00 a.m. They finished patching the dam two hours later. But the damage was done. The massive amount of radioactive waste traveled a total of 80 miles (130 km) downstream. The wastewater backed up sewers. It contaminated drinking water.

CONSEQUENCES FOR THE NAVAJO NATION

The Church Rock dam failure was the largest radioactive waste disaster in US history. It was especially disastrous for the Diné people of the Navajo Nation. The Navajo Nation covers about 27,000 square miles (70,000 sq km) across Utah, Arizona, and New Mexico. Much of the land is desert. The Diné people living there rely on the Puerco River for water. The uranium contaminated

In 2009, Joe Shirley Jr., the president of the Navajo Nation, gave a speech on the thirtieth anniversary of the Church Rock dam failure.

their soil and drinking water. It also affected livestock and crops.

Between 1944 and 1986, mining companies extracted more than 4 million tons (3.6 million metric tons) of uranium in the Southwest. Uranium mining reached its peak in the 1950s, and around 750 mines operated on Diné land. Today, many of these mines are no longer in use. Approximately 500 abandoned mining sites are still standing. When the uranium mines were abandoned, many were not properly sealed off or cleaned up. They continued to leak uranium even though they were no longer in use.

The Uranium Mill Tailings Radiation Control Act (UMTRCA) was passed in 1978. This federal law regulates the operations of uranium mines. It also provides guidelines for how to safely shut down these mines. Other US government policies have since been put into place to limit pollution from uranium mines. But many of these policies

URANIUM EXPOSURE

A study that began in 2000 shows that the Diné people have high rates of kidney disease compared to the rest of the US population. They also have much higher rates of cancer. Many experts think these health effects are linked to uranium exposure. Uranium can also affect blood pressure, reproductive health, and the body's ability to recognize and fight diseases.

The Moab Uranium Mill Tailings Remedial Action project began in Utah in 2003 to clean up uranium waste at a processing site.

were not yet in effect when the mines closed. The US government has made efforts to clean up some of the sites. But more than half of the abandoned uranium mines still have not been cleaned up.

For decades, the Diné people have suffered from poor health due to the contamination. One mining company paid $1 billion to the Navajo Nation for the damage. However, many local water sources remain

PERSPECTIVES

HEALTH IMPACTS OF URANIUM

Maria Welch is a Diné researcher who works for the Southwest Research Information Center. Welch's family grew up next to abandoned mines. They were exposed to uranium. Welch studies the present-day impact of uranium on families in the Navajo Nation. Her study found that 27 percent of her participants had high levels of uranium in their urine. This is true for only 5 percent of the rest of the US population.

For years, the Diné people did not know their water sources were contaminated. Many swam in and drank water with uranium particles. They washed their clothes in the water. Some homes were even built out of materials contaminated with uranium.

contaminated with uranium. In 2020, 15 percent of people in the Navajo Nation still did not have access to safe drinking water in their homes.

MINING'S IMPACTS

Mining is the process of removing metals, minerals, and other materials from the ground. These materials are used to make many products, including cell phones, televisions, and computers. There are many types of mines across the United States. Mining practices vary depending on the material being mined.

Mining affects the environment. The process of building mines and extracting materials can contaminate water sources. Land and vegetation must be cleared. Dust and chemicals can pollute the air. Mining and burning mined materials can increase the emissions of greenhouse gases. Large mines require a lot of energy and create a lot of waste. But there are ways mining companies limit and reduce their impact on the environment. This includes preventing pollution, minimizing waste, and establishing cleanup methods.

EXPLORE ONLINE

Chapter One talks about uranium mines in the Navajo Nation. The article at the website below goes into more depth about the effects of abandoned uranium mines. Does anything in this article surprise you? What new information did you learn?

ABANDONED MINES CLEANUP

abdocorelibrary.com/mining-and-the-environment

CHAPTER TWO

MINING'S EFFECT ON WATER

One of the main ways mining affects the environment is through water. Mining can impact water sources in several different ways. If an environment's rivers, lakes, reservoirs, or streams are polluted, the whole ecosystem is affected.

Mining waste can cause water pollution that harms plants, animals, and humans. In order to extract materials, large amounts of rock have to be removed. Sometimes the waste rock contains toxic metals like arsenic

Wastewater from mines can seep into nearby waterways. This pollution can take years to clean up.

and lead. These metals can wash into waterways. People and animals might drink the contaminated water. Eating fish and other animals that were exposed to the toxic metals also affects health. Exposure to these chemicals can lead to birth defects and cancer.

ACID MINE DRAINAGE

Acid mine drainage is a type of water pollution. It occurs most often at coal mining sites. Mining uncovers sulfides in the soil. These sulfides dissolve when they come in contact with water. When sulfides are dissolved, they become acids, which can wash away from mining sites and end up in waterways. Acid mine drainage can cause red, yellow, or orange sludge to build up at the bottom of rivers and streams. This is harmful to aquatic plants and animals. Acid mine drainage makes it difficult for wildlife to grow and survive. If not cleaned up, sulfides remain exposed at abandoned mines. Acids can continue to wash into nearby waterways for many years, even if the mine is not in use.

The Spring Creek Debris Dam collects and contains acid mine drainage from the Iron Mountain mine. It helps prevent mine waste from polluting nearby waterways and harming wildlife.

Iron Mountain is the site of a former mine near Redding, California. A company called Mountain Copper built a mine there in the 1890s. The mountain was mined for iron, copper, silver, and gold. As miners drilled into the mountain, they exposed a huge amount of a sulfide called pyrite. As pyrite in the waste rock dissolved, it led to acid mine drainage.

THE ROLE OF THE SACRAMENTO RIVER

The Sacramento River runs through California's Central Valley. It is one of the dirtiest rivers in the country because of mining. It has dangerously high levels of mercury. Mercury was exposed because of gold mining. It washed into the river. Mercury poisoning can kill fish. Eating fish that contain mercury can also lead to mercury poisoning.

For more than 100 years, the acid drainage and toxic metals polluted the nearby Sacramento River. The drainage from the Iron Mountain mine is some of the most concentrated acid pollution in the world. It is about 500 times more toxic than drainage produced by any other mine. The acid can dissolve fabrics and burn skin. The pollution killed thousands of fish. It was destructive for the Sacramento River habitat. The mine was abandoned in 1966, but the problem remained. The mine was not properly sealed off, and the water was not treated. Before cleanup began, one ton (0.9 metric tons) of acid water was entering the river per day. It made Iron Mountain one of the most polluted places on Earth.

CLEANING UP THE RIVER

In 1986 the Environmental Protection Agency (EPA) took over the cleanup of the Iron Mountain mine. The EPA worked to stop the harm from the toxins. It built a place to collect and contain the toxic runoff. After 20 years of work, 98 percent of

PERSPECTIVES

WORKING FOR THE EPA

Rick Sugarek works as an EPA project manager for the Iron Mountain site. He has been in charge of the cleanup for 20 years. Sugarek said, "Our main goal at the EPA was to protect the Sacramento River." Because of the efforts from people like Sugarek, the amount of toxic metals entering the river was largely reduced. The runoff can be captured and cleaned as long as there is funding available. But until the exposed pyrite runs out, no one knows how to fully stop the pollution at the source. Sugarek hopes that new technologies will put an end to the pollution.

Settling ponds near the Red and Bonita mine in Colorado collect water that is contaminated with metals and other toxic chemicals.

the toxic mixture had been contained. The quality of waterways around Iron Mountain has greatly improved.

However, the problem may never be fully solved. The pyrite remains exposed to water and oxygen. It will continue to produce toxic pollution. The pyrite will not completely dissolve for 3,000 years. The acid will need to be continually collected and treated.

Fortunately there are many ways to prevent acid mine drainage. Mine workers can add materials to wastewater that cancel out the acidity. They can also cover waste rock with topsoil and move waste to places where it will not contaminate water.

FURTHER EVIDENCE

Chapter Two covers the ways mining can contribute to the pollution of waterways and how this can be reversed. What was one of the main points of this chapter? What evidence is included to support this point? Read the article at the website below. Does the information on the website support the main point of the chapter? Does it present new evidence?

ABANDONED MINE DRAINAGE

abdocorelibrary.com/mining-and-the-environment

CHAPTER THREE

MINING'S EFFECT ON LAND

There are two main types of mining. Underground mining involves blasting tunnels deep into the ground. Surface mining involves removing material closer to the surface. This kind of mining creates large open pits.

About 1.3 million acres (526,000 ha) of federal land are used for mining. This is less than 1 percent of US land. However, mining still affects the land. Surface mining requires the removal of plants. It sometimes involves

Coal mining sometimes requires mountaintop removal, which can damage landscapes.

burning forests. Bulldozers, excavators, and other heavy equipment are needed to develop surface mines. These machines remove topsoil.

Some forms of surface mining use a method called mountaintop removal. Miners use explosives to blast off the top of a mountain and get to the coal underneath. The discarded rock is then pushed into waste dumps. This is common in the Appalachia

PERSPECTIVES

CONSERVATION IN APPALACHIA

Tierra Curry is a conservation biologist. She helps save plants and animals in danger of extinction. Curry grew up in Appalachia. She is familiar with the negative impacts of coal mines. She says, "I grew up playing in a creek and hiking in woods that were later destroyed by coal companies." Curry watched coal companies strip the mountains. Mining contaminated families' well water and covered everything in coal dust. She wanted to protect the mountains she loved. Curry says, "Protecting endangered species and the habitat and climate they need to survive helps make the planet healthier for everyone."

It can take billions of dollars to restore land to how it was before it was mined.

region, which includes eastern US states known for coal mining.

Clearing land causes erosion. Vegetation holds soil in place. When trees and plants are removed, the wind can blow away soil and nutrients. Rain also washes nutrients away. This erosion makes it hard for plants to grow. It also increases the risk of flooding. Soil erosion can lead to polluted waterways.

Mining can also lead to soil contamination. This means the soil has high amounts of metals and chemicals. This negatively affects plant health.

SALAMANDERS

Salamanders are very sensitive to their environments. Because of this, scientists can use the number of salamanders in an area to measure ecosystem health. A large number of salamanders can indicate a healthy ecosystem. A team of scientists studied salamanders in West Virginia. They found that salamanders were healthier when they were farther away from mining sites. Reclaimed mining sites had fewer salamanders than areas that had never been mined.

HABITAT LOSS

Wildlife habitats are destroyed when forests, mountains, and vegetation are cleared. This loss of habitat harms many species. Some animals are killed as mines are developed. Reptiles, amphibians, and small mammals are not very mobile. They cannot always escape the mining equipment and forest clearing.

Some species can recover from population decline, but it takes a long time. Others do not recover. Mining is one of many forms of human development that puts stress on wildlife. Houses, roads, cities, and landfills all reduce wildlife habitat. This overall loss of habitat can even lead some species to extinction.

RECLAMATION

Once mining companies have finished mining, they are required to help the land recover. This is regulated by the Surface Mining Control and Reclamation Act (SMCRA). This federal law was passed in 1977. It oversees how surface mines are started, operated, and closed.

The process of restoring the land after mining has stopped is called reclamation. Reclamation includes replacing soil, planting crops, or restoring habitat. A fully reclaimed mining site means that all threats to the environment due to mining have been removed. It also means that the mined land is given a positive use. For example, one mining company in California turned a mining pit into a strawberry field. A former phosphate mine in Florida reclaimed the land by bringing in healthy soil and creating wetland, prairie, and forest habitats.

HOW RECLAIMED LAND IS USED

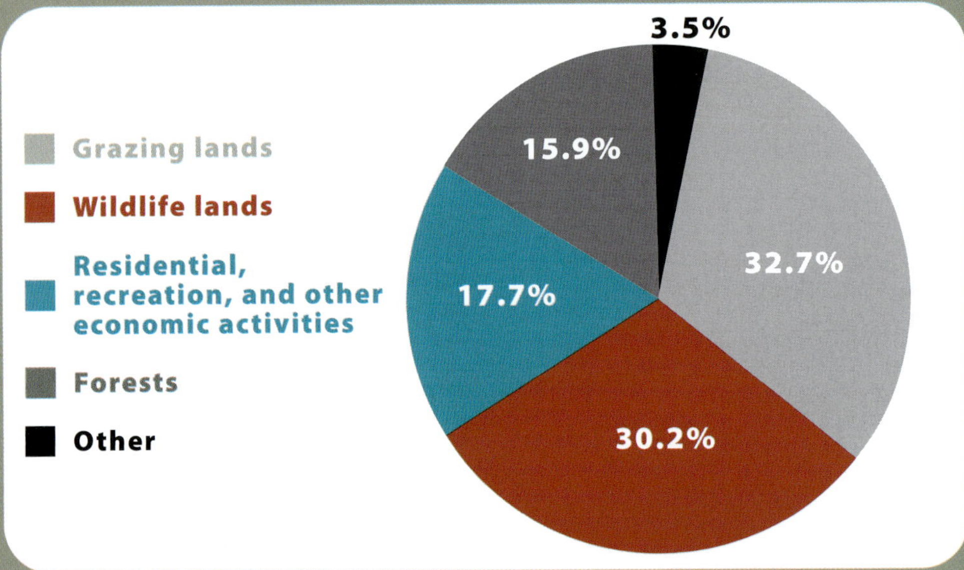

In a study published in 2018, reclaimed land was used for different purposes. What do you notice about the use of reclaimed land? Are these places mostly natural spaces or commercial areas?

Mining companies set aside money to cover reclamation costs. But sometimes reclamation is more expensive than planned for. Mining companies occasionally go bankrupt. The US government then has to pay for the reclamation. Many mining sites still need to be reclaimed. These abandoned mines continue to be sources of pollution.

STRAIGHT TO THE SOURCE

The Surface Mining Control and Reclamation Act (SMCRA) was the first federal law to address land reclamation after mining. Earl Brandy worked for the US Department of the Interior. That year he made a statement on the thirtieth anniversary of SMCRA:

> *During the mid-1970s, most counties in the Appalachian coal fields were dotted with hundreds of small surface mines. . . . I saw streams choked with sediment, and spoil and rocks dumped on the downslope in steep terrain. I witnessed the results of unpredictable blasting events and saw the exposed highwalls and abandoned entries that were left behind. These failures to reclaim the land resulted from many failures in the system that existed then. . . . It was these conditions that were to be addressed by SMCRA, which was enacted by Congress in 1977.*

Source: Earl Bandy. "Surface Mining and Reclamation." *US Department of the Interior*, 25 Apr. 2016, doi.gov. Accessed 26 Oct. 2022.

WHAT'S THE BIG IDEA?

Take a close look at this passage. According to the author, why was SMCRA necessary? What was its purpose?

CHAPTER FOUR

MINING'S EFFECT ON AIR

Mines release waste into land and water. Mining can also cause air pollution. Dust and toxic waste can become airborne as miners and mining equipment dig. Air pollution includes dust, dirt, soot, and smoke. Severe air pollution is visible as smog that makes a landscape look hazy. Some particles that cause air pollution cannot be seen without a microscope.

When particles that cause air pollution are inhaled, they get into humans' lungs

Dust from mines can become airborne. Spraying water on the dust weighs it down and helps prevent air pollution.

and bloodstream. This can cause health issues including lung and heart disease. The people most affected by air pollution are children, pregnant women, and the elderly.

COAL DUST

Coal mines release more than 17,000 tons (15,422 metric tons) of airborne particles annually. Studies have shown that people who live close to coal mines have higher rates of cancer than those who live farther away. Deaths from heart, lung, and kidney disease were also much higher for those who lived near or worked in coal mines.

Coal dust can settle on plants and block sunlight. This makes it difficult for plants to grow. The dust from mines also mixes with water. This reduces oxygen for fish and other aquatic species.

DUST STORMS

The Molycorp mine operated from 1920 to 2014 in Questa, New Mexico. The mine extracted molybdenum ore. Molybdenum is a grayish metal used to make parts of mountain bikes and wheelchairs. Nearly 300 million tons (272 million metric tons) of waste rock were removed from the mountain. Other mining waste was

The US government has worked to clean the area around the Molycorp mine since 2011 by removing waste rock and treating contaminated water.

transported through pipelines to lagoons full of acid waste. But the pipelines were poorly built. They often spilled waste into waterways and polluted them.

In the 1980s, dust from the waste rock began accumulating. Wind began picking up the dust, which contained toxic metals. Studies showed that the dust included lead, zinc, cadmium, arsenic, and mercury.

The citizens of Questa began to experience lung problems because of the pollution. Blinding dust storms started becoming more common. The dust burned people's eyes and throats. The 1980 state championship baseball game was supposed to be held at Questa High School. But the game was canceled. A dust storm made it too dangerous for students to play.

In 2009 the EPA declared the mine a Superfund site. This meant the EPA would clean up the area. But the Molycorp

PERSPECTIVES

CITIZENS TAKING ACTION

Roger Herrera raised his family in Questa, New Mexico. Herrera lived right next to the Molycorp mine. He was one of the citizens who fought against Molycorp. Questa citizens sued the company. They got the EPA to step in. They improved the health of the environment and of the town's people. Herrera says he thinks about the next generation. He says, "I want to see that they grow up in a clean, safe environment, instead of having their pockets filled with money with an unhealthy environment."

The EPA supervises cleanup efforts at Superfund sites, such as the Gold King Mine in Colorado.

mining company was required to pay for the efforts. The US government began removing the contaminated soil and rock. It also layered gravel and planted vegetation around waste sites to prevent the dust from becoming airborne.

One way that mines can reduce air pollution is by using water to keep work spaces damp and weigh down dust. They can also stop operations during windy or extreme weather conditions. By reclaiming land quickly and not leaving areas exposed for long periods of time, mines can reduce erosion. This limits the amount of dust that gets into the air.

SAVE
BLAIR
MOUNTAIN
ABOLISH
MOUNTAINTOP
REMOVAL

CHAPTER FIVE

MINING AND CLIMATE CHANGE

Climate change is a serious issue. Temperatures around the world are increasing because of greenhouse gases. Greenhouse gases include carbon dioxide, methane, and nitrous oxide. These gases remain in the atmosphere and trap the sun's heat.

If steps are not taken to reduce greenhouse gas emissions, climate change will continue to worsen. Effects of climate change include rising sea levels and extreme weather.

Increased concern for the environment has led to protests that aim to reduce mining in the United States.

Climate change can make it difficult to grow crops, which can lead to food insecurity.

THE SWITCH TO CLEAN ENERGY

Most of the greenhouse gas emissions in the United States come from burning fossil fuels. Natural gas, oil, and coal are all fossil fuels. The United States relies on these sources of energy for heat, electricity, and transportation. Approximately 79 percent of energy used in the United States comes from fossil fuels. Coal mining is a huge contributor to emissions of greenhouse gases. About 40 percent of global greenhouse gas emissions come from burning coal. The mining industry today faces pressure to reduce its effect on the environment and support clean energy.

In order for the United States to reduce greenhouse gas emissions, it has to use less fossil fuels. This means switching to clean energy that doesn't produce greenhouse gases. Some examples of clean energy are solar power, wind energy, and hydropower.

COAL AND ELECTRIC POWER

The United States relies on multiple sources of energy for electricity. Compare how much electricity coal produces with its carbon dioxide emissions. How does this help show the polluting effects of coal?

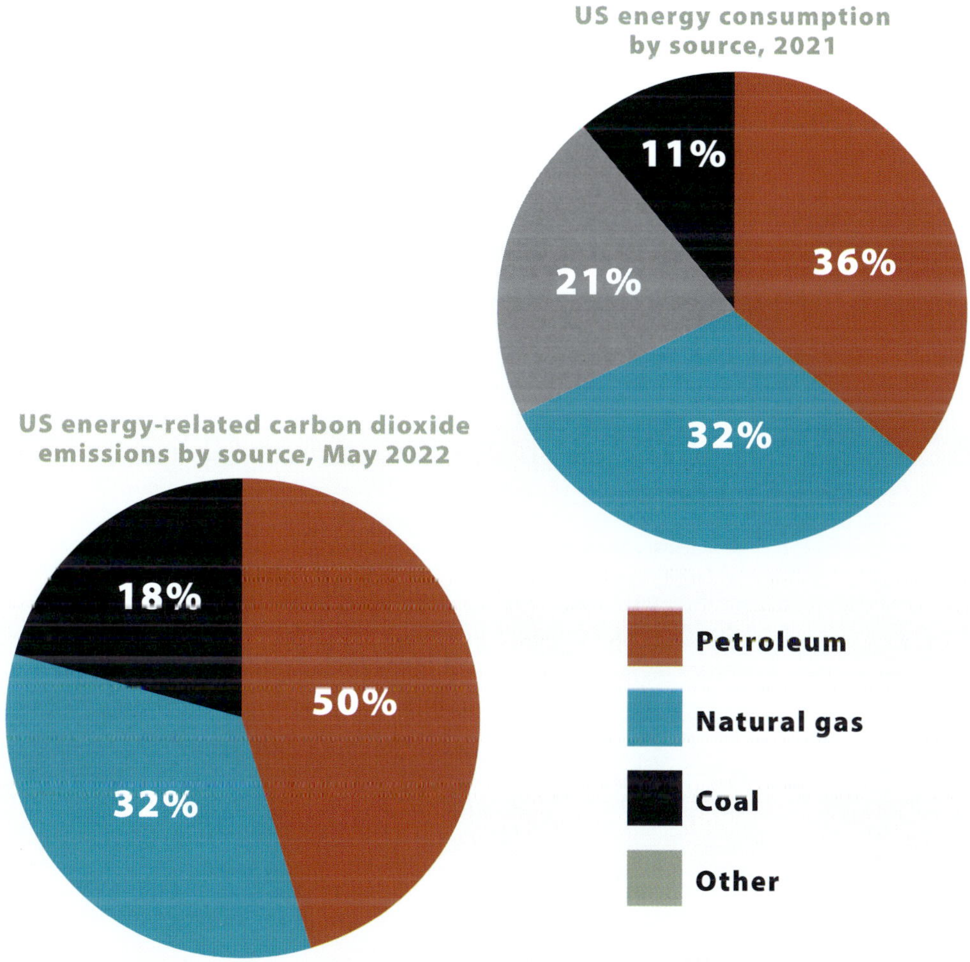

The equipment used to produce these forms of clean energy relies on mined materials, such as copper, cobalt, graphite, and nickel. This means an increased need for mining these materials.

CLEANING UP COAL

Carbon capture and storage is one way to reduce the effects of coal pollution. During this process, carbon dioxide is trapped before it can enter the atmosphere. In coal plants, this is done by separating the carbon emissions from other gases produced during the industrial process. The carbon dioxide is compressed and transported to a storage site. Often the gas is stored deep underground in rock formations.

SUSTAINABLE MINING

The global mining industry is responsible for about 4 to 7 percent of greenhouse gas emissions. But there are many ways to reduce this impact. One is to use clean energy during the mining process. Most mining equipment runs on fossil fuels such as gas or diesel.

In the future, mining equipment could be electric instead. Electric-powered equipment is better for the environment.

Many federal policies aim to reduce mining waste. More efficient removal methods, better storage and management of waste, and recycling waste for other uses are all ways to make mining waste less harmful to the environment. These methods limit pollution. Prevention methods

PERSPECTIVES

THE RIGHT DIRECTION

Scott Odell works for the Environmental Solutions Initiative at the Massachusetts Institute of Technology. He studies mining and climate change. He believes mining can be improved by enforcing regulations. Odell says that mining companies today are more willing to work with local communities and environmental groups than they were in the past. This collaboration is important for the future of mining and the planet. Odell says, "We need to respond to climate change, and we're doing that by transitioning to clean energy. But we need to recognize that producing clean energy has its own environmental and social impacts that we need to fix [at the same time]."

Mining companies and the EPA work to reduce the effects of mining on the environment. An EPA worker pours lime into water with acid mine drainage to get rid of the acidity.

are less expensive and more efficient than cleaning up waste. The mining industry can also continue to improve reclamation practices. The US government can help keep the mining industry accountable. People can support policies that protect the environment.

Mining can have long-term destructive effects on the environment. If not properly handled, mining can pollute waterways, soil, and air. It can also contribute to climate change. But the mining industry can make efforts to protect the environment. Through land reclamation, cleanup processes, and use of clean energy, the mining industry can reduce its impact on the environment.

STRAIGHT TO THE SOURCE

The International Energy Agency works with governments around the world to establish energy policies. It issued a press release in 2022 about a worldwide increase in coal use:

> *The world's continued burning of large amounts of coal is heightening climate concerns, as coal is the largest single source of energy-related CO_2 emissions. Worldwide coal consumption rebounded by about 6 percent in 2021 as the global economy recovered rapidly from the initial shock of the [COVID-19] pandemic. That sharp rise contributed significantly to the . . . increase in global energy-related CO_2 emissions . . . putting them at their highest level in history.*

Source: "Global Coal Demand Is Set to Return to Its All-Time High in 2022." *IEA*, 28 July 2022, iea.org. Accessed 14 Oct. 2022.

CONSIDER YOUR AUDIENCE

Adapt this passage for a different audience, such as your principal or your friends. Write a blog post conveying this same information for the new audience. How does your post differ from the original text and why?

FAST FACTS

- Mining is the process of removing metals, minerals, and other materials from the ground.
- Mining impacts the environment. It can harm the health of nearby people, plants, and animals.
- One way mining can affect water is through acid mine drainage. This pollutes water and causes problems for aquatic species.
- Surface mining involves the removal of topsoil and vegetation. This can destroy wildlife habitats.
- Once mines have finished extracting the material from an area, mining companies are required to help the land recover through a process called reclamation.
- Dust and toxic materials from mines can become airborne, leading to air pollution.
- Mining certain materials releases large amounts of greenhouse gases. These emissions contribute to climate change.

- The mining industry is working to reduce its effect on the climate. It does this by adopting more sustainable practices and supporting clean energy.

STOP AND THINK

Surprise Me

Chapter Two of this book talks about the effect of mining on water quality. After reading this book, what two or three facts about water pollution and mining did you find most surprising? Write a few sentences about each fact. Why did you find each fact surprising?

You Are There

Chapter Four talks about air pollution caused by the Molycorp mine near Questa, New Mexico. Imagine you are in Questa when a dust storm strikes. Write a letter home to your friends describing what you saw. Did the dust storm affect the way you feel about the mine? Be sure to include plenty of detail in your letter.

Dig Deeper

After reading this book, what questions do you still have about mining's impacts on the environment? With an adult's help, find a few reliable sources that can help you answer your questions. Write a paragraph about what you learned.

Another View

This book talks about mining's effect on the environment. As you know, every source is different. Ask a librarian or another adult to help you find another source about this topic. Write a short essay comparing and contrasting the new source's point of view with that of this book's author. What is the point of view of each author? How are they similar and why? How are they different and why?

GLOSSARY

ecosystem
a community of living things within their environment

emissions
substances released into the air, especially harmful gases

extinction
the loss of an entire species

habitat
the place where an animal or plant is naturally found

hydropower
the generation of electricity using moving water

pollution
the presence of harmful substances in the environment

radioactive
something that emits radiation, which is a powerful source of energy that can lead to harmful health effects

sulfide
a chemical that contains the element sulfur

topsoil
the top layer of soil with the most organic matter

ONLINE RESOURCES

To learn more about mining and the environment, visit our free resource websites below.

Core Library CONNECTION
FREE! COMMON CORE MULTIMEDIA RESOURCES

Visit **abdocorelibrary.com** or scan this QR code for free Common Core resources for teachers and students, including vetted activities, multimedia, and booklinks, for deeper subject comprehension.

Booklinks NONFICTION NETWORK
FREE! ONLINE NONFICTION RESOURCES

Visit **abdobooklinks.com** or scan this QR code for free additional online weblinks for further learning. These links are routinely monitored and updated to provide the most current information available.

LEARN MORE

Bédoyère, Camilla de la. *Hazardous Habitats and Endangered Animals.* Welbeck, 2020.

Ventura, Marne. *Mining Policy*. Abdo, 2024.

INDEX

About the Author

Emma Kaiser is a writer and educator based in western Minnesota. She has an MFA in creative writing from the University of Minnesota, and her writing has been published in a number of magazines and publications. She is the author of three other nonfiction books for students.